21st Century Skills Library

HEALTH AT RISK

ANOREXIA

Gail B. Stewart

Cherry Lake Publishing
Ann Arbor, Michigan

Published in the United States of America by Cherry Lake Publishing
Ann Arbor, Michigan
www.cherrylakepublishing.com

Content Advisor: Carolyn Walker, RN, PhD, Professor, School of Nursing, San Diego State University, San Diego, California

Photo Credits: Cover and page 1, © George Mattel/Photo Researchers, Inc.; page 4, © Lea Paterson/Photo Researchers, Inc.; page 6, © RDTMOR/Photo Researchers, Inc.; page 7, © Vidura Luis Barrios/Alamy; page 9, © David Young-Wolff/Alamy; page 11, © Spencer Grant/Alamy; page 13, © Paul Baldesare/Alamy; page 14, © Custom Medical Stock/Alamy; page 16, Maury Aaseng; page 17, AP Images/Ed Andrieski; page 19, © Jupiter Images/Alamy; page 21, © Mauro Fermariello/Photo Researchers, Inc.; page 22, © Ed Young/Alamy; page 24, © Chris Rout/Alamy; page 25, AP Images/John Heller; page 27, AP Images/Eugenio Savio; page 28, © BananaStock/Alamy

Library of Congress Cataloging-in-Publication Data
Stewart, Gail B. (Gail Barbara), 1949–
Anorexia / Gail B. Stewart.
p. cm.—(Health at risk)
ISBN-13: 978-1-60279-281-4
ISBN-10: 1-60279-281-X
1. Anorexia in adolescence—Juvenile literature. I. Title. II. Series.
RJ399.A6S74 2008
616.85'262—dc22 2008017496

Cherry Lake Publishing would like to acknowledge the work of The Partnership for 21st Century Skills. Please visit www.21stcenturyskills.org *for more information.*

Table of Contents

CHAPTER ONE

STARVING ON PURPOSE

A young woman rejects a plate of food. Anorexics literally starve themselves to death.

Anorexia is an **eating disorder**. The word ***anorexia*** means "loss of appetite." But it's much worse than that. If you have anorexia, you are actually starving your body. You are ignoring the hunger pangs that signal that your body needs food. You choose not to eat. As a result, you lose lots of weight. And the more weight you lose, the more you want to keep losing. Even if you become ill from losing so much weight, you don't want to stop. And this can be very dangerous—even deadly.

It's not always easy to recognize anorexia. You might think that all people with anorexia are skeleton-thin. But that's not always true. Doctors have a

Learning & Innovation Skills

Anorexia experts say that a large percentage of girls are too focused on weight. The next time you are with a group of girls at the lunch tables or on a school bus, listen to the conversations. How many times do you hear someone complain that she looks fat, or that she needs to lose weight? How many times does someone compliment another on how skinny she looks? Think about the reasons they are making such comments. Does the person complaining about being fat look fat? How do the people around her react?

When anorexics look at a scale, they cannot see real numbers, they just see "fat."

formula to help them decide if someone has anorexia. If you lose 15 percent or more of your normal body weight on purpose, anorexia may be the cause. Say a normal weight for you is 120 pounds (54 kg). If you keep your weight at 102 pounds (46 kg) or less, your doctor might be concerned that you have anorexia.

Anorexia is a confusing disease. It's hard to understand why people would starve themselves on purpose. Doctors say that people who have anorexia don't see themselves as

Even though anorexics are seriously underweight, they continue to see themselves as fat.

others see them. Even when they starve themselves to the point of being skin and bones, they see themselves as fat. They don't want to eat. And they don't want people to help them get better either.

It's hard to know exactly how many people suffer from anorexia. Experts think there are about 8.5 million people with anorexia in the United States and Canada. There may be another 2 million or more in Europe, Asia, and Australia. Anyone can develop anorexia. But most are young women between the ages of 12 and 19. Doctors are seeing more and more young people starving themselves to death. And that has many people very worried.

21st Century Content

Eva is 20 years old. She lives in Rye, New York. She has battled anorexia since sixth grade. She has been in the hospital seven times. Each time she promises her family she will start eating. But after she gets out of the hospital, she goes back to her pattern of not eating. The only food she eats each day is one-third of a banana and a few soda crackers. A normal weight for Eva is between 125 and 135 pounds (57 to 61 kg). But she weighs only 80 pounds (36 kg). Her mother, Corrine, says she is tired of worrying about her daughter. "I love her so much," she says. "But she is killing herself. And it seems like we are watching her die a little more every day."

CHAPTER TWO

THE CAUSES OF ANOREXIA

A thin young woman still does not like what the scale tells her. Anorexics do not have realistic views of their bodies.

21st Century Content

Besides limiting the food they eat, many people with anorexia spend hours exercising each day. They try to burn off even more calories to lose even more weight. Doctors say over-exercising is one warning sign that someone has an eating disorder like anorexia. Kris, a teacher from St. Paul, Minnesota, used to have anorexia. She says she would run eight miles every morning. "I didn't want my parents to know," she says. "They were already worried I was too skinny. So I would hide my running clothes and shoes in my backpack. I'd go to the high school track and run before school. If I didn't run, I wouldn't allow myself to eat anything that day—except sugarless gum."

There are a lot of reasons why young people develop anorexia. One common reason is that they want to fit in. They might hang out at school with kids who talk about dieting. They constantly count calories and skip meals. Before long, even if they don't need to diet, they go along. And pretty soon, they're losing weight they didn't need to lose.

Andrea is a 15-year-old from Vancouver, Canada. She developed anorexia in high school. She had always been a normal weight. But when she caught the flu, she was too sick to eat. She lost 15 pounds (7 kg). When she went back to school, her friends told her

Some teens who feel neglected by parents or do not fit in with their peers become focused on their body weight because it is one way of controlling or taking control of their lives.

how good she looked. "I never felt fat before," Andrea says. "But then I thought maybe I had been. So I started dieting to lose more weight. I liked the compliments."

A lot of teens starve themselves because they think being thin will solve their problems. That's how Margie, a

Learning & Innovation Skills

Many people have become concerned about the Internet's role in anorexia. They point to Web sites often called "pro-ana" (short for "pro-anorexia") sites. These sites often include message boards where people with anorexia can post updates on their weight loss. Some include photos of themselves. Some offer tips on how to hide their weight loss from family and friends. For several years, mental health organizations have tried to close down pro-ana sites. A new effort began in 2008. They worry that the sites glorify starvation. But some people disagree. They say that to close down the sites interferes with freedom of speech. They also say the sites give people with anorexia a place to communicate. Make a list of the pros and cons of pro-ana sites. What is your opinion?

12-year-old Minnesotan, developed anorexia. She was a little overweight. A few boys in her class teased her, and that hurt. "One day a boy called me Large Marge," she says. "I cried so hard. That same day I basically stopped eating, except for a little dinner. I thought if I lost weight, I would be happier. Kids wouldn't tease me. Maybe I'd be more popular."

Sometimes anorexia is a way to deal with family problems. Kids who have very strict parents or are unhappy for other reasons may feel that they have no control over their lives. That's how 15-year-old Cassie felt. She stopped eating breakfast and

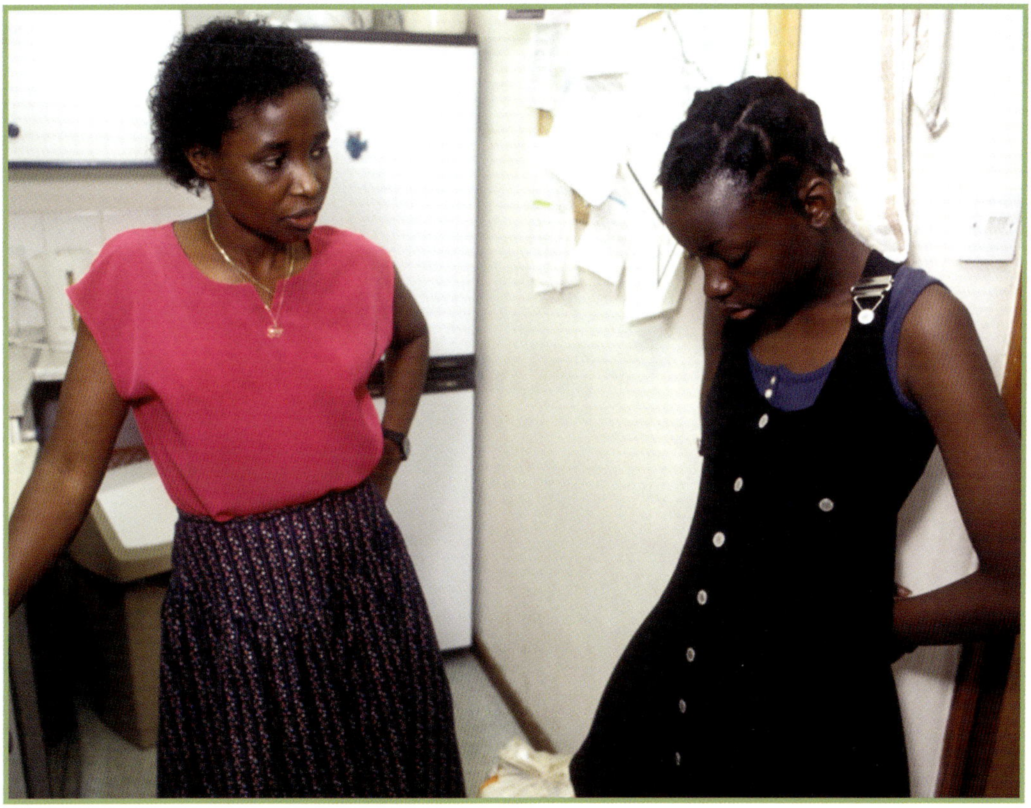

A caring parent or other confidante can help an anorexic get help.

dinner. She ate just a little at lunch. Her parents told her to eat more, but she told them she wasn't hungry. "They couldn't make me eat," Cassie says. "It was a good feeling, to make some decisions on my own." She thought she was in control. But she was actually making herself very sick.

CHAPTER THREE

A Horrible Disease

A young woman sees a distorted image of herself in the mirror.

When you have anorexia, you don't just lose weight. The more you starve yourself, the more damage you do to every part of your body. Your hair and nails will become brittle. Eventually your hair will begin falling out. When you don't eat enough, your body doesn't make the oils that keep your skin healthy. It gets dry and flaky. The palms of your hands and soles of your feet turn yellowish. Your skin grows **lanugo**, a fine hair, to keep your face and the rest of your body warm.

But the most dangerous changes happen on the inside of the body. When you starve yourself, your body shuts down to protect itself. To save energy,

Life & Career Skills

Body image is how you think about the way you look. Do you like your body, or are you usually worried or unhappy about how you look? Studies have shown that body image is formed when you are very young. Without realizing it, parents or older siblings may teach you that being critical of your body is normal. Imagine, for example, that you're watching your sister try on a new outfit. She criticizes how she looks in the mirror. She may say an outfit makes her look fat. What messages, if any, might that send to you? How might this affect you as you get older?

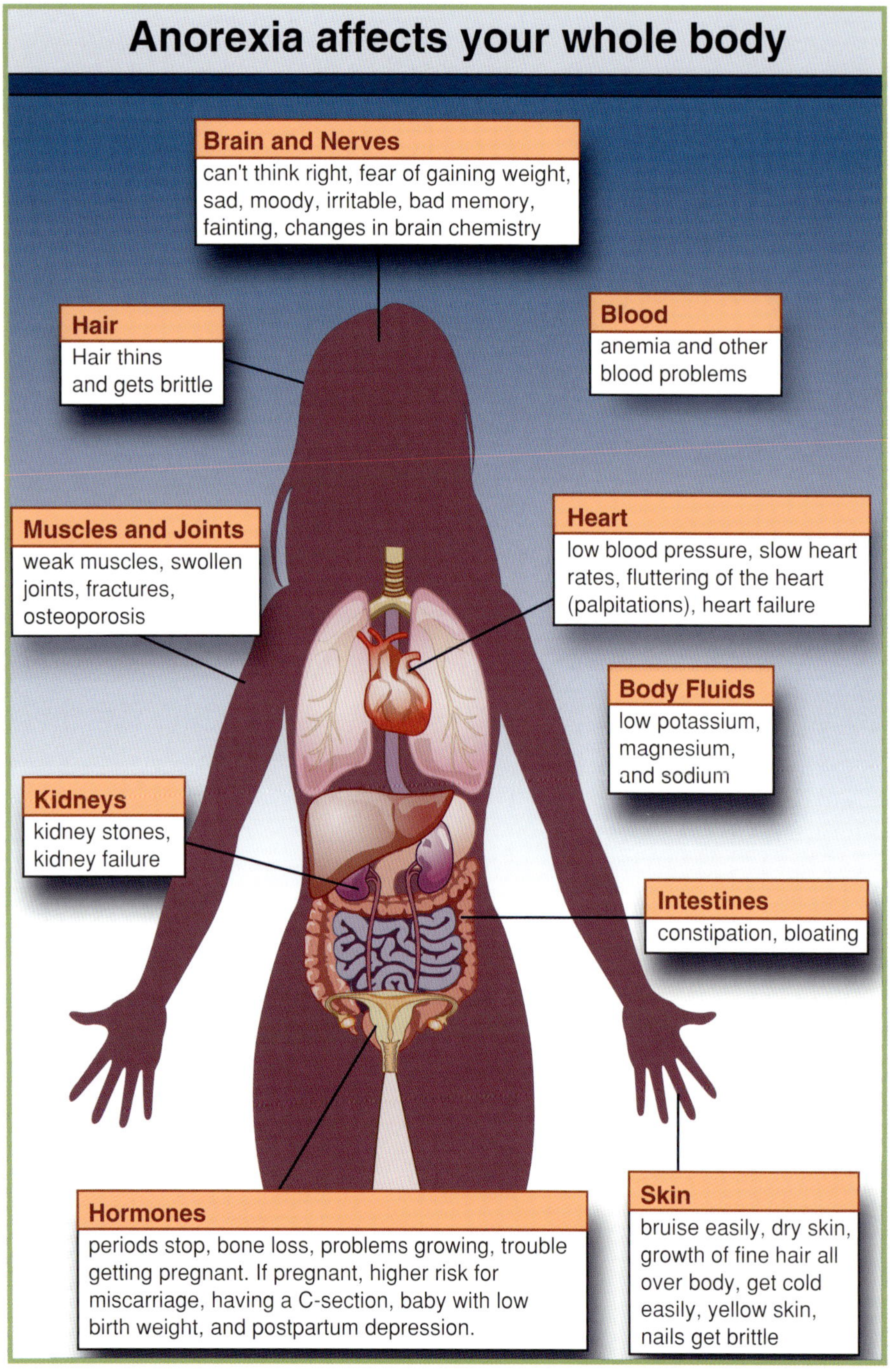
Anorexia affects your whole body
Brain and Nerves
can't think right, fear of gaining weight, sad, moody, irritable, bad memory, fainting, changes in brain chemistry
Hair
Hair thins and gets brittle
Blood
anemia and other blood problems
Muscles and Joints
weak muscles, swollen joints, fractures, osteoporosis
Heart
low blood pressure, slow heart rates, fluttering of the heart (palpitations), heart failure
Body Fluids
low potassium, magnesium, and sodium
Kidneys
kidney stones, kidney failure
Intestines
constipation, bloating
Hormones
periods stop, bone loss, problems growing, trouble getting pregnant. If pregnant, higher risk for miscarriage, having a C-section, baby with low birth weight, and postpartum depression.
Skin
bruise easily, dry skin, growth of fine hair all over body, get cold easily, yellow skin, nails get brittle

your heart rate slows. Your blood pressure drops. The body doesn't have enough calories to burn for energy, so it burns fat. When there isn't enough fat, it eventually starts burning muscle—including your heart muscle. This damages the heart. It can't pump the way it should, which can lead to a heart attack. Women with anorexia also find that their **menstrual period** stops.

Anorexics often do not understand that their bodies destroy themselves under the strain of starvation.

Some of the most frightening damage occurs in the brain. Anorexia changes the way you act and the way you think. You don't see that people are concerned about you. Instead, you believe they are your enemies, wanting you to be fat. You don't see how thin you have become. You don't see how much your body has changed. Instead, you look in the mirror and see a fat person. "It made no sense," says Sharon, the mother of a North Dakota girl with anorexia. "She eventually dropped to 74 pounds [34 kg] and she still thought she was chubby. I thought, 'How can we help her if she can't see what we see?' What a. . . [horrible] disease this is."

21st Century Content

Many people with anorexia have specific goals they are working toward. Sometimes it is reaching ever-lower numbers on the scale. Sometimes the focus is a particular part of their body. Kari, a girl from Wisconsin, had anorexia. She went to a group home to get better. "There was a girl there I'll never forget," she says. "She was focused on making her thighs as thin as possible. She wanted to be able to put her thumbs together and put her hands around the biggest part of her thigh," she says. "And her fingers had to touch. I remember she kept doing that, all day long, trying to put her hands together around the top of her thigh."

CHAPTER FOUR

GETTING BETTER

As part of the treatment, anorexics must weigh themselves and have increased weight goals to achieve.

Learning & Innovation Skills

The media is often blamed for making kids too focused on weight. Critics say ads using super-skinny models send the wrong message to readers. Go to your local library and page through two or three magazines aimed at teens—*Cosmo Girl*, *Teen People*, or *Seventeen*, for example. Choose 10 ads and separate them by the body type of the models. How many feature overweight models? How many feature underweight models? How many models look as though they are a normal weight? Why do you think the advertisers chose one body type over another?

Severe anorexia puts a person's life at great risk. After a while, the heart and other organs shut down. The person becomes too weak to survive, even when doctors try to help. But many people with the disease can be saved. Doctors say there are three steps in saving someone from anorexia.

The first is to get medical attention. Some people with anorexia realize they have a problem. They can go to the doctor and say they need help. But lots of people with anorexia refuse to do that. In cases like these, family members may have to force the person with anorexia to get help. Some people with anorexia have to be physically dragged to the

An anorexic patient receives counsel as she eats at a medical clinic. Hospital treatment is often required to make an anorexic gain weight, while psychotherapy may be needed to teach healthy eating habits.

doctor. In severe cases, doctors may put anorexics in the hospital. The second step is to start eating. This will help the body recover. Anorexics may not want to eat. So, family members have to make sure the anorexic is getting food.

An anorexic teen and her therapist look in the mirror as they work together to improve her body image.

Or sometimes people with anorexia are too weak to eat. In that case, they may be hooked up to feeding tubes. These tubes pump fluids with vitamins and other **nutrients** into the body.

Once they're stronger, they're ready for the third step in getting better. This is **therapy**. Just gaining weight does not mean the person is cured. It is important to find out what started the anorexia in the first place. Sometimes the therapy is one-on-one, with a **counselor**. Other times, it may involve a group of people, talking together about their similar concerns. Learning more about the problems that caused the disease is very important. Otherwise, the anorexic might go back to the same pattern of not eating. Unfortunately, even with therapy, many people do just that.

21st Century Content

Many people with anorexia also develop another eating disorder, called bulimia. People with bulimia rid their bodies of food they eat. Sometimes they force themselves to vomit right after eating. Other times they use drugs like laxatives to give themselves diarrhea—another way of getting rid of food. Bulimia has very dangerous effects on the body. Constantly making yourself vomit can be deadly for the heart muscle. The acid from vomit rots your teeth. Frequent vomiting can cause bleeding sores in your stomach, too.

CHAPTER FIVE

Everybody's Problem

A teen girl worries that she may not measure up to the ideal figures she sees in the fashion magazine she is reading.

Anorexia is becoming more common every year. Many doctors say they see younger and younger people with the disease. Some children as young as six or seven are starving themselves on purpose. The National Eating Disorders Association reports that 40 percent of children in grades one through three wish they were thinner.

Research analysts Lorraine Swan-Kreneier, left, a psychologist, and Tasha McGregor take a seminar to train them to investigate the role of genes may play in anorexia.

Scientists are working to discover why some people get anorexia and others don't. Some say there might be a **gene** that makes certain people more likely to get the

21st Century Content

People with anorexia get very good at hiding their disease. Even so, there are several common warning signs that may alert other people:

- unusual interest in calorie count of foods
- wanting to eat alone
- beginning to miss menstrual periods
- exercising for long periods of time
- making negative comments about his or her body

disease. If so, that information could help families watch for early signs of anorexia. Stopping that behavior early could mean the difference between life and death.

But there are already ways for people to fight anorexia. The media can really help. Ads showing super-skinny models give young people the wrong idea of what's beautiful. "Fitting into size zero jeans should not be anyone's goal," says one counselor. "Our society is sending unhealthy messages to kids. So many girls with normal bodies look in the mirror and feel like failures."

Parents and other family members are even more important in fighting the disease. Supportive family members can

The French parliament introduced a bill in 2008 that would make it illegal to "publicly incite thinness" after a model with anorexia died.

A supportive family is crucial to helping teens negotiate difficult times realistically.

help you through problems or stress. They can help you see that what's inside matters more than how someone looks on the outside.

Other kids can help, too. It's important to remember how powerful words can be. A mean remark to a classmate can hurt more than you know. But kind words and friendship are healing. If you think someone may be struggling with anorexia, talk to her or him. Or tell an adult what you suspect. If you are wrong, that's OK. But if you're right, you may save a life. Anorexia affects individuals. But the solutions are everyone's business.

21st Century Content

Most of those who suffer from anorexia are female. But boys can get anorexia, too. Experts say that about 10 percent of people with the disease are male. Some of these are boys who have been overweight. They may have started dieting and then found that they enjoyed watching the numbers on the scale drop. Even when they become too thin, they don't want to lose that sense of accomplishment. Another reason boys develop anorexia is that they are in sports in which weight is an issue. These include running, swimming, or wrestling.

Glossary

anorexia (an uh REX ee uh) an eating disorder that causes people to starve themselves, usually resulting in weight 15 percent or more below normal

counselor (KOWN suh luhr) a professional who helps people who have personal or psychological problems

eating disorder an unhealthy, extreme concern with food, body image, and eating

formula (FORM yoo luh) a method of calculating healthy and unhealthy weight ranges for each age

gene (JEEN) the basic unit of heredity, the information passed from parent to child that determines the way the body looks and works

lanugo (la NOO go) a covering of soft downy hair that grows on the face and body of people with severe anorexia

menstrual period (MEN stroo ul PEER ee ud) several days during each month when a nonpregnant woman's body sheds the bloody lining of the uterus

nutrients (NOO tree uhnts) substances that provide nourishment for the body

severe (suh VEER) very bad or dangerous

therapy (THARE uh pee) counseling or treatment to cure physical or psychological problems

For More Information

Books

Arnold, Carrie. *Next to Nothing: A Firsthand Account of One Teenager's Experience with an Eating Disorder.* New York: Oxford University Press, 2007.

Orr, Tamra. *When the Mirror Lies: Anorexia, Bulimia, and Other Eating Disorders.* Danbury, CT: Franklin Watts, 2007.

Radev, Anna, ed. *I've Got This Friend Who: Advice for Teens and Their Friends on Alcohol, Drugs, Eating Disorders.* Center City, MN: Hazelden, 2007.

Redd, Nancy Amanda. *Body Drama.* New York: Gotham, 2008.

Web Sites

Food & Fitness, KidsHealth.org

www.kidshealth.org/teen/food_fitness

Dozens of articles for teens about healthy weight, body image, and eating disorders, including anorexia.

Mirror-Mirror, Eating Disorders Shared Awareness (EDSA) Canada

www.mirror-mirror.org/eatdis.htm

Anorexia information includes recommended reading and directories of national organizations and treatment centers all over Canada.

National Women's Health Information Center

www.4women.gov/faq/easyread/anorexia-etr.htm

This site has answers to a range of frequently asked questions about anorexia. It also provides advice for people who suspect that a family member has the disorder.

Teenage Health Freak

www.teenagehealthfreak.org

This Web site covers health issues that are important to teens, including issues related to body weight and personal relationships.

Index

About the Author

Gail B. Stewart is the author of more than 220 books for children and young adults. She is the mother of three sons, and lives in Minneapolis, Minnesota.